MW01094255

Class

Deonte Osayande

Crossroads Poetry Series
Detroit, Michigan, USA
Windsor, Ontario, Canada

First Edition. February 2017

Library and Archives Canada Cataloguing in Publication

Osayande, Deonte, author
        Class / Deonte Osayande.

(Crossroads poetry series)
Poems.
ISBN 978-1-988214-11-5 (paperback)

        I. Title.

PS3615S26.C53 2017   811'.6   C2017-900336-4

Book cover design: D.A. Lockhart
Cover Image: Hommage à Rivera @ Detroit by SoupStance (Flickr)
Book layout: D.A. Lockhart

Published in the United States of America and Canada by

Urban Farmhouse Press
www.urbanfarmhousepress.com

The Crossroads Poetry Series is a line of books that showcases established and emerging poetic voices from across North America. The books in this series represent what the editors at UFP believe to be some of the strongest voices in both American and Canadian poetics. Class is the sixth book in this series.

Printed in Adobe Garamond Pro font

To Destiny
Thank you so much
and I hope it inspires
your own writing.

Deonte Osayande

Contents

I:

II:

I.

The Paranoia Says the Helicopter Searches For Me

as the announcement
of the training
exercise on campus
for the police force comes
into my classroom and I joke
about the threat, about
my blood pressure as if
there wasn't a shooting
at a community college
weeks before, as if I weren't
the same complexion as the targets
cops use at their shooting ranges.

Translation

Margaret immigrated here last summer
from Nigeria, says she saw my name
and decided to take my class
not knowing how I'm a half truth. She reminds me

of my unauthentic nature
without trying to. Although I'm a deception

translating the radio static everyone else hears
when she speaks English isn't difficult. She proudly
tells her classmates how to correctly pronounce my last name

accurately shares the origins
of my deceit. She says my first name has no meaning
in her hometown
and my homeland says the same

about my life. I'm packaged with plastic popcorn, protected
but still breaking, alive yet still fragile. I want to apologize

for the boys in her hometown
who didn't reach my age, for the boys
in my hometown who didn't reach my age. Nobody hears

how sorry I am since the thought
never migrates outside of my mouth.

Expectations

I.

After the fourth week a student sneaks in
their grandson so they can see me. I am
a dragon. I don't exist on their planet. We share
the same world but until now he has never seen
anything quite like a version of him ten years away.

II.

The next year someone brings
their mother. I am a circus

attraction. The only thing here
out of the ordinary to be seen. I recognize

the mother from the line of people
in the grocery store days earlier.

III.

A student says they recognize me. I bought
my phone from them a year before.
She doesn't remember it, the faces

come and go like obituaries. She swears
I look like someone she saw
on a t-shirt her friends wore once.

IV.

Every staff meeting I become the moon,
apparently beautiful to look at, catching
the attention of my coworkers who sit
away from me. I'm alone. Only the one professor

who taught me at another university years before
comes over to my table. "Young, intelligent, black
and alive" she says. "You know, from their perspective
it isn't personal. None of them expected you to be here.

You still look like a student." I've found the trapeze
which I walk on. I've discovered how I'm the phantom
formed from a thousand headstones. My existence
sparks the imagination, defies all expectations

like escaping the gravity of my environment.

Alchemy

On the first day of the semester I'm disguised as a student,
hoody over my suit and tie, asking everyone enrolled
in the class about the professor, about the textbooks. This prank,

a magic trick I can only pull off once a semester. Before
class starts I shed my camouflage and explain how despite my class
being on literature they will also learn alchemy. This

illusion is the first lesson in my class. I am this black body, something
often referenced when filled with lead. I turn lead into gold.
Valuable. Black bodies, no matter how they're dressed, in a suit

or hoodies and sweats, valuable. We use alchemy
to cure ailments, dissolve substances and transform metals. Every day
is a holiday, a celebration for not being dead yet. There are

four key elements in alchemy: earth, water, wind and fire and the ether connecting
them all. A student asks why we connect so many worldly issues
within the classroom readings and I refer them back to the elements:

graves, alcohol, smokes and guns and the ether connecting
them all. We are products of our environments. Systematically more people
get buried in this earth than plants and it's no wonder

everyone grows so depressed. Women become wind, disappearing,
and like them protests for them pass on. I've seen many people
lose lots on slots, gambling since there are more casinos than empowered

politicians willing to address why their address
lies outside of their jurisdiction. Those in office don't care about
our blues, just getting green and revenue. Business bosses

become guns firing people like bullets in the hands of young angry
adults. A student says he doesn't care about the oppression
others in the world have to face, asks why we connect so many worldly issues

within a literature class as if what we read and write isn't effected
by what we live, as if it isn't all alchemy. As if addiction isn't an illusive
internal illness influencing our desires to dissolve substances

into our systems. As if addictions aren't ailments to be cured. As if every
time innocent people are shot it isn't a transformation of metals,
a change in connotation. As if our bodies aren't meant to be golden.

Blackout at Cody MCH, Detroit 2014

I'm exhausted, breaking up
two girls fighting in our classroom.
Released early, I'm solemn,
bright sparks shower on city streets,
firearms firing works
at young onyx bodies;
a silent hunting
no off season,
no bounty.

By the time the news
reports reach the television
more of them drop
to the asphalt.

Names not given, business as usual.

I'm still in my apartment,
silence harbors my hiding,
a form of escape. I pray
for myself,
for these kids,
I pray
we learn to be elusive.

I look out my window
at the lost and unfound
search for the glass ceiling
we're trapped underneath.

Masks

I teach poetry as a means of survival to endangered species.
My black students laugh wildly in the classroom
but when I asked them to write what masks they would wear
they grew silent as trees falling in forests nobody hears,
wondering if changes of face could help them live longer.

My students write about their personal disappointments,
about how they're a generation of premature martyrs,
about how their skin is this weird hybrid camouflage,
about how nobody notices them until they are dead.

They know their lives are treated like fields of grass,
nobody says they see a problem with them being cut short.

They are becoming the foundations of gardens,
black girls and boys buried before blossoming,
broken bodies bearing bullets below their bones.

I know how they have trust issues instead of trust funds,
nobody is banking on their survival. They are not safe.
I know how they are a generation drowning in silence.
I know how it feels to be living invisible when we are dying.

My face is just a mask. It fools my mirror.
Tells it I am older, as if that means I'm a survivor.
I own the man it hides underneath,
the one who hears the horrified sound of endangered children,
falling like a forest.

I know how a shotgun on a porch
turned a young girl asking for help silent.
I know how a pistol on a watchman
choked a young boys sweet tooth with his own blood.

I know this classroom is only a reservation
I know how it is hunting season,
outside we are considered big game
by people with guns calling us threats.
I teach my students everything I know in these poems
as if I'm not still on the run with them.

Suspension at Gompers Elementary, 2011

Anthony has a gunpowder filled mouth
and his words shoot out
during a test, distracting his classmates. After he's handed

his first failure. He says he hates me
as if I haven't faced hate before. The other teacher in the room
calls his dad, sparking spanking anxiety

and while the other students go to lunch I sit with him
to try to stop his fear from eating
at him. I say I'll teach him magic tricks. When I was his age
nobody taught me how easy disappearing was. School

yearbooks, history textbooks, all smoke and mirrors
in the way black faces vanish
when you get closer to the present. I explained

how we were once called crows, how a group of crows
gets called a murder, how boys like us get murdered
and if we survive we get are systematically grouped
transformed into birds in cages, tricks used to make money.

Orbit

On this one day I asked my second grade class a question
about circles, using the planets

as an example. This one kid, William, sits there, staring
at my face as if he was eager to pounce. I stop my patrol

around the room and ask for his answer.
His quivering lip says nothing and I wait for him to speak

until he suddenly starts crying. When consoling him
in between his sobs, he says he had to use the bathroom

and couldn't hold it anymore and at that moment I realized
I had been watching him pee himself. The friend I'm telling

this story to laughs like a meteor shower crashing
into the moon before he says I'd have to eternally be a kid

to be that clueless. If only it were that easy, if only my joy
wasn't defined by children I have yet to father.

My first love had her first child recently. I wanted to say
more than congrats, to say the infant's eyes, the greatest

gift I'd ever seen, to say I hope each morning is as good
as grandma's breakfast on a Sunday. Her family, a growing

flock of hallelujahs. Her family, an orbit I don't foresee
breaking, a life between her and her husband spent

like a heavenly dance twirling in a room full of stars. I wanted
to say all of this but I'm carrying too much

of this lonely. I'm cratered
with envy and embarrassment. Even Pluto,

divorced from it's solar system
of a family has a moon still married to it.

Sunrise in the Mourning

The other students told me
he didn't make it. I rushed
into the bathroom, finding Demarcus

crying, sitting in a urinal of his own
shit, right next to the stall. In a way I also
couldn't contain myself
and I became a comedy club

laughing at this second grader. So close
and if I had let him cut in line
he wouldn't have needed new clothes. We reached

the front office with faces drenched in heavy rain
as our laughter became booming thunder
alongside each flash of a smile
crashing between the tears. I tell my nephew this story

knowing how they would be the same age now. My nephew asks
why bad things happen to innocent people. I am answer bankrupt,
creating debts, explanation empty, funds gone. I try telling a joke

to distract him since I don't have an answer
outside of how I worry about my students, and their families,
how difficult it must be parenting
hunted children. The joke goes like this,

death is a roommate who always moves in
unannounced, always borrowing what he doesn't plan on
giving back. The punchline is our rent stays paid

with our lives especially when different denizens are deceased
daily. Today I grieve the dead still living. I fear
watching the news and seeing familiar pictures, recognizable

names. I'm afraid for these students. Genocide is a sunrise,
someone always wakes up mourning.

As I'm Telling the Story About the Time I Burned My Chest

Falling on the track at full speed everyone's eyes gravitate
towards the football game on the TV behind me, their seismic
shift in attention shows how shaken they are seeing this rookie

wide receiver with my same name
make his first professional catch. They thought
I made him up. Nobody believed me when I told the story

about getting gifts in high school from a university
who thought I was him. None of the scouts
checked close enough to see if they had the guy

they were looking for. Everyone here
notices my smile as the evidence
of what I recounted comes out. My friends think

my stories are often more entertainment
than scene worth investigating. I tell everyone
another one, how I learned manners

from playing Perfect Dark on my Nintendo Sixty Four, how
at the points where characters aren't shooting the shit
out of each other they exchange pleasant greetings. Nobody

believes me until I put in the game to show
them. Everyone here knows how much
time and effort my mom put into trying to teach me to act

acceptable, like I have home training. It didn't work. I know
how I am viewed. It's pointless. No amount of manners can convince
people who only see expendable when they see me to change

their minds. Coaches and threats both
lead to trails of broken bodies so often I'm not surprised
how nobody feels guilty over it. I've seen so many

men like me fall apart for the profit of someone else, so many men
dying with life still in their bones, so many die
for nothing. Sometimes I want to talk

about them instead of myself but I don't have enough time to tell
all of the stories. Someone
asks me to talk about the first time I ran

after a train I needed to catch. I can't, my urgency
lost. I grow tired of all the times
I've almost caught bullets and bullets and bullets.

In College I Knew a Guy Who Kept Suggesting Coffee Would Cure Me

as if swallowing more blackness
could right the chemical imbalances
of my brain. Once, when I was sitting

in disability services I could have sworn
he called me a nigger as if I'm not some type
of bear but the word that left his mouth

was lazy. He said it because I was an athlete. He said
he thought black people were supposed to be strong,
not disabled, as if we can't be both. He thought narcolepsy

was a good excuse for extra rest and a note taker,
thought I made it up
like a child's sighting of the sandman. He called

the world my pillow, as if people don't normally die
by what gives them comfort: drinks, drugs, sleep. He didn't understand
how much hard work it took getting a math degree

when I'm a calculator constantly counting sheep. He persisted
in trying to tell me how to cure the parts of me he thought
was too disabled to be black. Can't I be the bear

and still have the winter in my blood? Can't I hunt
and hibernate? Do expectations for me have to stay
slept on? Sometimes, when people call me lazy

I think I hear nigger, broken slave for sale
auctioned at a discount. Don't hire him
he can't work right. Can't work, right? I think

of Harriet Tubman, fighting for her freedom
through the sleep episodes, constantly
going back for more people. One time in college

I saw this guy passed out at a party. Maybe
from drinks, from drugs, I don't know, he wasn't
one of the people I would go back for. I'm not

his shepherd after all. I'm not counting on him
looking out for me. He didn't know how hard it is to pass,
to look so "normal" when my body is made out of sand.

Pitbull

I.

In a drunken rage he turns pitbull,
frightens his girlfriend
into a submission of silence,
assaults a mutual friend of ours,
made me rabid, foaming frustration
which had been boiling over
for all of the months we lived together.

When all is calmed
his hangover is more
throbbing knot from blow
than one drink too many.
I apologize, he doesn't
remember the cause
only the pain. His best friend,
offers an ice bag as consolation.

II.

His best friend says the stupid Nigger did it,
with a tone which echoed underneath his skin
for generations before he was born.
He doesn't realize he said it
as if there was a courage in
being disappointed in his country
for finally electing a president
who doesn't have the same old skin tone.

My roommate does the most composed thing
I have ever seen erupt from his impulsive frame.
He politely asks his best friend to leave our dorm.
After his guest leaves he looks to me
with the same riot in his eyes
pulsating through my own.
In that moment he apologizes to me
on his comrades behalf with more shame than sincerity.

III.

On a night, quiet as his father's presence during his childhood
my roommate sits across from me weeping. He doesn't know
what he is doing in this downward spiral called a life.
He has used reverse gravity on all of his friends.
His girlfriend has been treated as expendable.
He wears the scent of the other women, doesn't even hide it.

It is fitting, that when she tosses his things from her window
she doesn't hide his adulteries from the other women.

His own mother treats him like the boy who cried wolf.
Her phone is always lost when his name is on screen.
He has reached his breaking point. All he has left is me,
and I've grown tired of living with him, I'm obligated to be here.
The room where he finds sanctuary is my sanctuary as well.
He says his best friend called him a beast as if he wouldn't miss him dead,
as if he would be first to tie the noose, as if he has a white hood in his closet.
He said his best friend said this with a hiss, as if he had been a snake all along.

IV.

My roommate gets kicked out.
Turns the room into New Orleans in 06,
New York in 01,
Detroit in 67,
Greenwood Oklahoma in 21.
He leaves no *fair well, goodbye,* no apology.

He stayed loyal to his best friend like a pitbull
since they were in high school in Grosse Pointe.
Loyal until the end, when the leash was cut,
and his side was kicked. Last thing I said to him,
was you're going to be alright dawg, I may not like you
but even I see good in you. I didn't mean to lie.

Holden Hall Dorms, 2008

We called him horse when most
called him Jersey either
because he was from New Jersey

or since he frequently wore them. The rest of us
in the dorms knew him for different reasons, for

the day he left his dorm door open
with his computer on his favorite genre of porn.
The asshole a couple doors down cut up the volume

loud enough so everyone could hear his guilty pleasure
and as moans and neighs echoed through the hallway,
he rushed back to his room blushing in embarrassment

to hide his hatred for us all. I felt sorry for him
until the weekend when he had called a girl a nigger
at a frat party as he tried to insist he could fuck

her better than any man had before. The next morning he tried
damage control, apologizing to her, my girlfriend, and to me,

by slipping a letter underneath her dorm room door. She already
had told me what happened by then, but he expected retaliation,

violence, a stampede of fists, a bucking of knuckles
against his mandible. This is how white fear works,
like an overhead projector, covering human beings

with perceived images and fears enough that the actual person
becomes difficult to see. As a black student athlete, in his eyes
it was a matter of time before I would revert into one of the beast s

he called us in private, or while carving hate filled hieroglyphs
into the walls of bathroom stalls. Filled with fear, it wasn't long
after he slid the letters under our door before he dropped out

and moved back home, worried I would be so thirsty for revenge
that I would tell everyone his secret. The morning he slid the letters
under the door I bust my ass slipping on them as she laughed so hard.

Phantom

The movie you both went to see isn't important. How
this date leads to the car, to the windows
fogging is what matters. Initially neither of you notice
the phantoms, the white men
who have been watching you, the way
both of your black bodies become a show
and isn't that American. To invade the space
black bodies occupy without question,
as if they belong in front of whomever watches. Now
you and her witness how you both became the entertainment,
against your wishes for people you will never know. The anger
takes your breath away, heats up, fogs the windows
on the way home. On the way home you are both silent, haunted.

Sink

We talk while I'm washing the dishes, questioning
the strength of our friendship, protesting
her date with him, because
of how he attempted
to force himself
on my ex-girlfriend
years before. The plates
never come clean. I scrub
but the memory of the sins
he attempted won't disappear. A glass
breaks in my grasp, blood on my hands
if I don't bring the reason I don't talk to him
back up. The pots stop getting washed when she
calls to tell me how he showed up at her home uninvited.

When Insulted on the Internet by a Racist I Realized This

sardine to a submarine, he didn't come up
on my radar. I didn't fear the supremacist
behind the keyboard, I was surprised
because I knew him from college
but I didn't truly know him
how I thought I did. He
was a glass car
who thought he had
illuminated headlights, hateful
beliefs and ideals. I told my father
about the comments he made online
in an attempt of character assassination.
My father told me "I had finally made it."

Mascot

Inside the mascot suit, a hot and dirty
personal purgatory everyone else enjoys
on the outside. Antics alone are enough

to warrant the laughter of small people presently
in attendance for the spectacle, not slightly
concerned about who you are underneath. How heavenly

it must be to come out of the suit. To lose all of that praise, to hear
the prayers of spectators no more, to represent nothing
when losing divinity, the culture forgets who you really are

over time. Gods and beliefs are forced into competition, the sport
of destroying bodies. One does it to the athletes
while the other does it to followers. Isn't being a god just

about bearing the burdens of man? Isn't it
like being the mascot of a culture, a sharing
of victories and defeats forgotten over time.

The Token

At a dinner in one of the high class hotels downtown
the waitress looks familiar. When the two of you
get a chance alone in the hallway you catch up
briefly on what you've been doing since
high school. Before rejoining
your table she asks how
you got invited
there. She asks
if you noticed you
were the only black one
there who wasn't part of the staff,
if you knew you were their way to pay

the token.

Detroit Yacht Club, 2006

On the balcony above the riverfront, she listens
to me speak about the year before and says
"it must have been nice getting to bring someone

you love." while thinking of her own forbidden
girlfriend. She thanked me for asking her to come here
with me on my second time at prom. Years later

after the sex change, he'll bring it up when we're recounting
our memories from high school. He'll ask if the rumors were true,
if during my first time at prom I took Crystal Johnson to the balcony

of the yacht club so we could dance underneath the moonlight.
I confirmed it, and at that time we thought we would stay
together for the rest of our lives, and taking her to prom

was the coolest thing I had done my whole time in high school.
As we sat on the balcony I explained
how it was never about the acceptance of the other

seniors around her, it was about making her mouth
warm with an unforgettable smile, our tongues
hot with hunger for each other. During my second time

going we spent more time talking
about the timelessness of that dance
than either of us spend enjoying this one.

Handling the Fragile

In high school my hands were boxing
gloves when I played the violin. I've never been

good at handling the fragile. When holding
my best friend's newborn I don't know

if I'm filled with more, hope, joy
or anxiety. I'm a concert of broken eggs. A carton

of more noise than music settling
within my own head. I want

children of my own but I think too many
griefs have impacted my smile. There are people

I would want to meet my first kid who already
can't, people I can speak to but that I can't

hear from anymore. Because of age, or cancer,
or violence. When I hand him back

his son
I crack.

Barrel

I knew I hated him. I knew they said
people where I'm from are like crabs in a barrel, constantly
pulling each other down. I know his name

isn't important. I cared
about Shanna, how this girl I had a crush on
pronounced his name so right it could have been said

on the news. This is when I knew she was dating
him and that on top of how he jumped me in the gym
bathroom a month earlier was enough

for me. I knew envy, I knew wrath, how they often go
hand in hand like he and I on the same team
exchanging the relay baton. It didn't matter when we came

back from our high school's first regional track meet. These boys
from the neighborhood around the school came for blood. It didn't matter
how lioness Coach Jordan was, guarding us

like cubs, her loud roar got silently caged
when the jackals aimed that tool
of trigger and lead at her. I couldn't see it, my limbs

were busy becoming shields protecting the boy I wanted
dead a month before. A rumor I heard
said the limbs on the tree on the side of Timberland boots

used to be used for hangings and I don't know
how true that is but I watched the tears sway from that boy's eyes
as an overcast of stomps rained down on us both. I heard

someone say they turned the barrel towards us
but I didn't see it, I was busy pulling that boy down, underneath
my guard. I lost track, confused

about which one of us
was supposed to be
the crab at this point.

The Day Shareef Took My Seat By the Door

My name was not yet a threat. My name
was not yet an invitation to hear

about family members who went
to serve in the war. My name did not yet

reflect the heritage I descended from.
At the time my name was just

another absent mark turned late
in the attendance booklet, another whisper

among the other students, speculation
and rumors about cultures

outside of their own. My name
belonged to a black kid in their eyes.

My name was foreign but still American
in a way to them. My name was still

defined in the inner city to them. My name
didn't change their perceptions of me instantly

on that day like it did Shareef. When walking in
my first hour my religious studies teacher

didn't call my name, didn't finish attendance, never
clarified how real everything on the TV was, the planes,

the explosions, the rubble and sounds of people
screaming, running. We were supposed

to watch a movie that day, discussing
what we saw afterwards. I didn't realize what I witnessed

until years later, recognizing the expression Shareef had
on the face of someone else accused of being a terrorist

for no other reason but their name. I didn't fully understand
what I witnessed until I was accused for the same reason.

Yearbook

You haunt this house, with
your maroon uniform, shoulder

pads the width of an axle. I only recently
got rid of your shoes. You linger

here where I stay. You whine about
if anyone will like you, worrying about being

late, as if it matters. Clocks pay you
no mind, your time already up. The girl you were

so eager to see doesn't remember your name
anymore. A ghost, with more urgency

than it needs. I can't shake
you or any of your mistakes

from me. The gun someone else stashed
inside your locker. Your silence

when Jasmine came to you for help. The fist
fights in the bathroom. I tell you nothing but your complaints

stay in my ear, an echo rattling inside my head. I want to tell you
life goes on, but you don't know

that you're not here anymore. I thought you were lost
with the yearbook. I pretended that you

never existed until I found your student ID. When I looked at the picture
I saw myself. Regardless of how much hair

now warms my face, how much muscle
rests on my build, I'm still growing out of you.

Virtually Deadly

They didn't know I was black
the first time I got called a nigger. We played
video games online, the one place

where black boys fire guns
without becoming instant monsters. While winning
the match I didn't realize what fires waited

inside of us boys until I made the victory shot
on the kid on the other end of the internet, releasing the poison
from his viperous tongue. I didn't have a mic

when I was online, which is to say I didn't have a voice
to hurt him with any power my words could possess,
which is to say I found myself blacker than I knew

as unheard as I always had been. Minutes
later came the second time, from a couple
of teammates, as a term of endearment, a thanks

for covering their backs, acknowledgments
of a good job listening to orders. I'm certain
they didn't know I was black, didn't know

how insulted I was, but I'm also certain they wouldn't have
cared so long as I continued to follow orders. At that time,
I was one of the best at my favorite online shooting games,

which is to say pulling triggers no question, following
orders, more comfortable with real and fictional death
than my own blackness. When confronted with the story

of Joan of Arc, I cried like the Catholic schoolboy I was.
Let the news report another victim of violence who looked like me
and I wouldn't flinch. Today I've been listening:

I have veterans for friends. I know how quickly our country martyrs us,
how it burns us at the stake when returning from war, instant monsters
if owning guns without ever targeting other black bodies

while following orders. I know how loud the unheard cries
against the violence are. I know how comfortably snakes sleep
at night, aware of our deaths. I know this isn't a game.

Time Capsule

I. *Icarus Speaks of Angels*

They will say how I fell into the ocean, but I was never afraid
of the sea. I had visions of many things
in the water. I saw generations
of young boys like me with ancestral

feathers tarred onto their bones. Many of them
trying to shine. Many of them
dying before their time. Their fathers are much
like mine, imprisoned, trapped

in mazes of iron bars. The ocean appears
to be a time capsule,
all these centuries
later.

II. *How Many of Us Must Fall*

before enough is enough? How many
times do youth have their names forgotten

unless they become obituaries? Please
don't let me name the children

unless you want them to hate us before
they become teenagers. I can't promise I'll come up with

something that won't cause difficulty in getting job
interviews, how employers won't want to try

pronouncing their names right, how nicknames will become
identity assimilation, as if it wasn't hard enough.

III. *Things You Missed, For Mike*

Move in day. Meeting your first
roommate. Meeting what would have been

your future wife. Meeting
your future.

Football players treating their families
worse than balls of pork skin. The fall of Cliff

Huxtable. Epidemics that weren't
until they crossed the Atlantic. Every beheading

that wasn't important until it happened
to someone that crossed the Atlantic. The World

Series. Protests from Palestine to China. The domestic army in your backyard. Another you
in cosplay. Another you buying a BB gun. Two more

of you in Missouri. The lack of arrest. The abundance of unrest. The state
of emergency. Your parents on the hip hop awards. Your parents

speaking to the United Nations. The way
their sadness was colder than the snow.

The Loss of Innocence

In public schools the first time boys fight
they're just boys being boys. Little intervention,
just suspension since the system doesn't want to see

their faces. In a different school system, where
most of the other children don't
favor minority appearances or backgrounds, everyone

mispronounces names, borrows traditions from other
cultures. Innocence is an imaginary friend. The authority defines them
as a threat, doesn't believe in boys being boys when black

anywhere except behind bars. It isn't about education anymore
but money, blood, industry, and business. School test scores
become blueprints for jails, schematics for imprisonment. More

suspensions and expulsions and how does taking children away
from their education as a punishment
for being disruptive of their education work? The idea isn't

for them to learn but for their eradication. When
the death doesn't come soon enough
the mayor transforms into a U-haul, systematically

moving us out of our homes. The governor gives residents
toxic tap water, filling the children with lead since cops

can't cap kids quick enough. We get emergency managers
who only manage to create emergencies. The last time urban boys

fight is usually for their own breath, rarely knowing
what they're up against. How many bodies

can one administration pack
into boxes for the U-haul? Misplaced memories

like the innocence
of our youth. The imaginary friends

become forgotten
like broken appliances
in the garage,
like old clothes,
like vintage traditions,
photographs
of the dead,
names
of the dead,
the justifications
of genocide,
political shepherds
making excuses
scapegoating
the victims
of their bigotry,
how many
people
were punished,
without crimes, the boys
who became half men
half sheep groomed
for the slaughter,
the loss of innocence.

II.

Class

First economics lesson, comparing
what's outside the bedroom windows
with what's witnessed in movies,
and shows and everywhere else. Media

dictates perceptions, shows the definition
of lower class represented in mirrors, not
on televisions. The upper class remains
talked about by the many, but not lived

out. Second economics lesson, observing
the textbooks older than the teachers
at the public school with chalkboards which
happen to be the only option around

until understaffed, until budgets become
weeds waiting to be cut, until the eventual
closing. Third economics lesson, being
told about the social construct of race

as if class were natural, and not based
off of invented concepts. Most living things
don't need structures in order for them teach

or learn. Most living things don't need division
based on the idea of trade and consumption. Roses

are classy and dandelions are weeds, despite
the fact that both need water and light
to survive. On the way to dinner, I pick up a bouquet

of flowers, neck held within a Windsor knot. Door held
open while entering the restaurant. Shared laughter
over lobster. Waiter tipped, well. A gentleman. On the way

home, pulled over. Watched and questioned
before the Sheriff says he feels threatened
but I'm a gentle man. He calls for backup, but I'm classy. I did

nothing wrong. My roots don't even reach this area
often. I was just,
wandering, now I'm wondering if this is how I pass

but tonight I'm lucky enough to survive for another day. On the way
to work the fountain I walk past
becomes a wishing well. I throw fourteen pennies in.

fix the classes, fix the lessons, fix the teachers,
fix the principals, fix the schools, fix the districts,
fix the cities, fix the states, fix the countries,
fix the world, fix poverty, fix politics,
fix economics, fix the classes.

The social construct created in our heads,
explaining how it never happens to be about
race always about class and economics. Before I start

teaching a pupil comes to me, his crying overflowing
past the brim of his glasses. This

tearful student feels filled
with guilt over the running from oppression

he rarely faces, finally realizing the racist
way he thought it was always

only about economics when each incident wasn't
isolated. I had heard about a homeless man, shot
and killed on the street, on camera. I had heard

about a college student, brutally beaten
on camera. I had heard about a famous basketball player, leg
broken outside of the club on camera. Classes change
but the suspect subject matter stays the same.

Pantheon

Let schools be shrines, praised
and where children are
praised. My grandmother has one

in her own name down south
in Tennessee where she taught
before our skin was allowed

as students. My pantheon
family needs no altar. We're divine
entities in the lost faith
of believing in the schools. My father

has many ruins, sacrifices, temples
littered around my hometown. Fairbanks, Pembrook,

so many closed schools, abandoned congregations
where my father was the principal
praised by parents. It's all forgotten now. Even he
can't recall the names of his students when he sees them

like prayers still waiting for an answer. It's all forgotten now
as the blessed things tend to be, as the holy things tend to be.

Eulogy to My Grandmother

and it begins with the sinking
of the unsinkable. You and the Titanic
dwelt around the same time,
yet it has only seen the underworld.
Haven't you as well?

When you left you had seen
the first great war and renaissance,
depression of drought and despair,
and the creation of clouds of men,
the napalm and marches, hoses
and assassinations, addictions
and dances,
humanity's cataclysmic calamities.

You had seen the sky fall and all
of this and much more, you had seen
it all while black. While black as well,
the view like from the bottom of a well,
a light above is what you had seen
within the depths of you,
unsinkable.

Praise

the ghosts of carcassed homes,
the mother, cook, who fed her family
from the kitchen that now belongs
to the growth of small bushes.

Praise to the father, worker,
who's office space now has a sunroof
for a ceiling, the whole second floor
once warm, now a collector of olden snow.

Praise the children, the only ones,
still alive today, which doesn't change
the fact that they are ghosts. Their bedrooms
are now a birdhouse in the home they left behind.

Praise the dog for never leaving, even when
his family told him to go. He buried his bones
in the backyard. His own bones are buried
in what's left of the living room.

Praise the construction crew, archeologists of our time,
for not tearing it down, for recognizing
the beauty of the abandoned, because all things human must die
isolated. Although that is never really the case, now is it?

Pensacola, 1998

A child on a pilgrimage,
I was with my family.
Seated in the center of legends
when I met my elders.

There had to have been at least
Five centuries totaled up in this room.
All the ancients of my bloodline
sat there and spoke with us.

There wasn't a single Adam's apple among
them, just a bounty of ribs to serve.
My forefathers had been forgone,
matriarchs missing masculine heroes.

All that these women
nurtured and mothered
over the years,
returned to see them one last time.

Their husbands had long rested
by the water because
even when we grow old
we die young.

Our men, when still boys
have already run out
plenty of sand
in their clocks.

Figurines of dads long gone
still linger behind welled up eyes
when they see us. Amongst all of their descendants
they look so alone.

Anxiety

There are no birds on the power lines
filled with shrapnel and debris. Yesterday

My arm was a hammer. Dad found a body.
A friend of mine
is more of a living casket, now that he's back

from active duty, drinking as if each swallow
were a Molotov cocktail going down

his throat. I don't know
how to comfort anymore.
I'm becoming collateral damage,
a jar full of fireflies no longer sure
if I'm trapped or if there are
tiny flames moving around inside me. I laugh

explosions, my eyes broken dams. I'm eclipsed
by my own anxiety. When anyone asks how
I'm doing, I don't know if they want the truth.

I spend my evenings searching for constellations
I can't name. I know stars are memories
of a universe too big to forget them. Every time

I love someone their struggles
become a bursting of light, a ghost
of concern sticking with me. I never forget,

even
when they become fog, when
they become knives in my shoulder
blades, shrapnel in my arms, a casualty
of war sitting across the dinner table, a missing
person now found, still missing from their family.

Each new year I feel a new talon tugging
on my arm. I have no power left. I want to do something,
but unlike a new year
there are no resolutions.

Battleship

My niece asks a barrage of questions
as I teach her how to play

battleship. With each missed
shot she takes the seven seas around me

ripple unsettled, rocking
me from sight to side, tidal waves. C4.

How come you don't have
any children? Miss. A1.

When are you going
to get married? Miss. I8.

I heard you say your doctor said you're losing
weight. Why don't you eat like you used to? Miss. H8

If you want to move out
why haven't you yet? Miss. D5.

Why do I hear the other adults in the family
asking you to take medicine? Hit. D6. Is there something

wrong with you? Are you sick? Are you going
to be alright? Hit. D7. When we have dinner

why do you stay in your room
to yourself? Hit. D8. Every time one of my mother's friends

has a new baby you want to hold them. Do you want
to have one one day? Hit. D9. My daddy said

men aren't supposed to cry. My daddy isn't around
much but you are. I've never seen my daddy cry but I've seen

you do it when you laugh. Are there other times when it's alright
to cry? Hit. D10. Why did you stop going out with your friends? Why

have you stopped doing anything that isn't staying
at grandma's house? Why do you get upset

when I ask so many questions? Hit.
You sank my battleship?

The Magician Remembers the Disappearing Act

We thought you were dead.
When I broke the news to her,
it broke her.

After five years you show up
to our brother's funeral.

Two months after you disappeared
a swelling cauldron of a woman appeared,
looking for you. She left a message,
said, "*She was keeping it.*"

At family reunions, one child
disappears from the photos,
He always searched
the albums, looking for
a ghost of a man
who has never been there.

He's in the den
looking at pictures of you,
staring, caught
between who he is
and trying to regain
who you might be.

Today

Today, I brush my teeth until I draw
blood that isn't mine. I've swallowed
so many names belonging to the dead. When

asked how I'm doing I want to say don't come
to me for water. My hole in the ground
hasn't been dug yet. I'm not well. I can't recall

if I've washed my face today. I'm not the morning person
I want to be. I shower with sunlight
in hopes that I will grow out of all of this

which I have become. I'm not the mourning person I want
to be. My sister did with her life what quarterbacks get paid to do.
My sister did what speeding drivers do to slow cars

on the highway. My sister did what good students do
in their favorite class. That is to say I've never been taught
how to handle when someone passes. I shy away

from most people these days, as they smile
like poachers and I'm the elephant in the room. I want
to believe them when they say everything will be alright

but I just become a filled water cooler around their casual
conversations. Despite how many of my buttons will be pressed.
I won't shed a drop. I won't lose my layers, I won't shed a tear

like I want to. I won't become old brakes screeching. I won't
be a hammer punching through walls like I want. I'll swallow
it all again, like a hole in the ground, like the well unseen.

Stand Up Until the Guns Stop

We stand here ready to battle to the death
in the living room of my home. I'm armed
and you are loaded with only the claws
that a squirrel could have. I know it's you.
We first met when I was shoveling snow
a day ago. You were digging for your nuts.

The woman upstairs screaming in fear of you,
my mother, days before looked her best friend
in the eye as she told her she fears I will never marry.
Her friend wonders why, while my mother looks at me
in a way saying she has seen me love a lot of broken.
In that moment I felt as if I were a cracking field of ice.

I've always been an ice cube inside of an oven,
failing at keeping cool. My temper has died down
but winning over the approval of others has never been
a point of success. Once I flirted with a girl by mentioning
that cows have best friends and they become seriously stressed
when they don't see each other for long periods of time.
Not a great way to reveal insecurities while eating steak.

So why tell this to a random animal that has broken into my home?
Last night in my headphones I was listening to stand up comedians
while the neighbors turned our street into guerrilla warfare.
I laughed until the bullets stopped, a peaceful madness of sorts.

Here you are, a fellow survivor of their guns, but a trespasser no less.
The violence no longer startles us like the thirtieth time you've seen
the jerk of neck from an Alabama tree, and we're from there. You

are making my mother jump like the first time she witnessed
a weapon. One of us has to go, and I believe I was in this home first.

Chess

During the week when the Cleveland police department got away
with killing a 12 year old black boy I was teaching my nephew

who was the same age as the murder victim
how to play chess. Police and prosecutors persecute us

over our actions like pawns to be punished
by the privileged. We keep thinking

about the actions of others ahead of time, considering
the absence of consciences or consequences
against the knights of the law when they destroy

every attempt at navigation across the boards
where we live. During the week
when a Texas police department was cleared of charges
in the "suicide" of a black woman
under their watch I was teaching my niece

how to play checkers. When confronted
by the law we can end up trapped, murdered bodies jumped over

despite how wrong the man with the badge is, despite
the lies they tell, despite how many ways
crimes weren't committed
except for living while black. A woman moves

across the board, like a queen
as far away from where she started as she can
and suffers the same fate as the king

who still lives where he grew up. I'm trying
to teach the kids in my family how these games work

but every day someone like us is checked, taken
while the majority of white people I know
pretend that they aren't playing. They have fun with us
and leave when we start dying, doing nothing to help

like bishops telling us to offer forgiveness
when we are too dead too often
to know what we must forgive.

Fear & Forgiveness

My mother prays
for the hate
to be removed
from the hearts
of so many
in this country
before I realize
how we lack
even somewhere safe enough
for us to do that.

Dagger

My mother used to be an English teacher, my father used
to be a principal that could teach math. You would think I'd do a better job

calculating my words but often I'm suspended in time
as anything comes out of my mouth

like a blade I didn't know I had. I've inherited
my father's sharp tongue. He doesn't realize how he cuts his family

with his words. One summer I found his machete he owned
underneath all the junk in the trunk of the car

he passed down to me. When I asked about it I learned
about the concealed dagger in his mouth. I doubt he would know

what I was talking about if I were to bring it up
now. We are stressed desserts but the dementia keeps

flipping his hourglass memories out of place. When he conveniently forgets
or gets upset my mouth gets dry. I don't want to talk, and I mostly

avoid him altogether as an angry heat
rises in me. He gets quick to find criticisms, accuses my mother

of affairs, shames his grandchildren on their weight, and once
fired a home healthcare aid for stealing something

he actually lost. I'm losing my father to his own mind, and I'm handling
loss like someone trapped in a revolving door, forgetting

to push forward. Our relationship stagnates. I avoid him, knowing
how every time he swings his swords of words around me

I lose my cool and remind him how many blades are in my mouth. I remember
the cracks in his armor. I remember how to cut but I keep forgetting

his condition, forgetting how each verbal barb can be what replaces a memory
he once had. He never asked for this and for all I know he could have inherited it

from his father long before I was born. I let my words become sharp
as the wind of a sandstorm and push him away, forgetting

how the first step to stabbing
someone is to simply come close, and push forward.

Passed Down Practices

It calls my name,
the whiskey.
The odd thing is
we have never met.
It makes me wonder
how it knows my name,
how I can understand
what language it speaks.

The Liquid Dragon Speaks of Ares

I've watched my dad disintegrate,
a wicked legend
acting like a stranger

in the house he built. There is no easy way
to tell a man they treat beer
bottles like shining suns
and their sons like bottles
easily recycled. Honestly I love him

but he is the reason
I learned how to hold a broken women
long before I learned how to kiss one. I know
how this legend is supposed to end,

with a confrontation
and then replacement. His demons
make him drink
while mine steal away my sleep. The fire
stays in his chest, but I am quick

to spew out glacial lava. My tongue
can make men burn, and freeze
at the same time. I'm not biting at the hand that fed me
I'm trying to let it know I can feed my self. I don't have time

to fight my father or his demons,
because if we were in the wrong location
there would be a witch hunt for us both.

On the Porch

I'm showering the floor with dandruff like my father
before me. Flakes of his nightmares
fall from his scalp fifty years after he had them

when I explain different current
events to him. When he was young he thought the hoses,
beatings and curses he had to endure

would be enough of a sacrifice so I wouldn't have to face
them today. My dad is like his country, old,
stubborn and being wrong is a harder pill to swallow

than the medicine he needs because of his age. Now it's sundown
and we're sitting on the porch with combs scratching our heads raw
searching for the answers, for the right

words to say. Neither of us can find them. When nightfall
finally comes neither of us can sleep. He sleep
-walks, unaware that he's eating all of the food

in the house again. I'm left laying there
with the television turned on to cartoons. Elmer Fudd chases
Bugs Bunny. He says "be very very quiet, I'm hunting" and in this

moment I think Elmer would make a great politician, trying
to ease the public to sleep, to convince
people that they shouldn't say anything

when death happens on his watch. The next
time I talk with my father we discuss finances, laughing

when I open my empty wallet, a whale carcass

stuck to the bottom of my dried ocean of a pocket with
nothing in it but enough pennies in it to make
barrages of well wishes. They never come true.

Method Acting

Every day a stage, Oscar worthy
performances. How my own family can't tell
when I'm acting, thinking

everything is fine and without drama. If only
they knew about the theatrical productions
going on around them. The ill don't get trophies
for living with what hasn't been cured

but forget about awards anyway considering
how the sickness in my head wrote the script
instead of being treated. I'm staying in character

whenever others are around. The drain
unplugged, pipes behind my pupils burst
whenever I'm alone. Faulty water mains wait
beneath my cheeks, behind the action

of making everything appear alright. I've watched
so many others audition for the same part as me

including many of my relatives. This skin I've worn
becomes the costume when in front of any audience.

There hasn't been a day since the new year began
when I haven't been on the set. Depression is a director
of movies with all of the same endings. Our memories
become the film, projected and replayed in our heads
when it's too late and we regret what could have been.

Even now, in this poem
acting in character
for so long becomes too much
and the exhaustion tucks away
my secluded sadness
into my blankets
only for me to wake up
in the middle of the night
if I'm lucky enough
to have not taken my final bow.

Letting the Monster Live

In this horror movie the black guy doesn't die. He isn't gone
within the first few minutes. He isn't the cool best friend
to the main character. He isn't comic relief given

since now the movie is in an urban setting. The setting
actually doesn't matter: street, school, hospital, police
station. This time the black guy is the killer, America's self imposed

fear and false cliché. Stick me anywhere and he can appear. This form
of black on black crime, both new and the recycling of old
tales easy to recognize if they weren't swept underneath the rug

like a mystic curse nobody cares to break the cycle of. The possibilities
for sequels are endless. At the end of the day, all
horror films are about survival and there will always be struggles

for survival between the monster my depression has become
and I. Wherever I go he follows and we both
know our conflict only heads in two directions: if he lives, I win

to be tormented another day but if I die, he wins. My depression
wears the face of who looks back at me in the mirror
and it wouldn't be so bad if it didn't carry a cleaver of my worst sins

with it when it jump scared into my reflection. Every surprise appearance
reminding me of how easily I can be found when there is no way
to hide from myself. Being the killer in a horror flick isn't easy

when you're also the victim, constantly chased
by a magical apparition you can never get away from. I have become

part escape attempt, part trap. He knows

all of my best hiding places, turns concealed chameleon, murders
my trust in family, scalps relationships with a knife of insecurity,
chokes out friendships with a chain of neglect. My only

option is to do what almost all of the horror movies do,
have a happy ending and win despite the catch
that comes with it. The monster never really

dies and so long as there's a protagonist to pursue
the sequels are endless. I'm not the only black guy running
from this beast so the remakes are endless. So long as nobody talks

about the haunting
the horrors will continue
to chase us to our graves.

Terminal Ethnicity

Being diagnosed with terminal
ethnicity prevents many students

from completing their assignments
on time since
they are serving
time   customers   their country

and everyone thinks they can see everything
they need to know from their
record   clothes   skin   name

instead of how they are tested
        in class outside of class
                at work at home
                        with friends   with family.

Everyone assesses how
        threatening   talented   intelligent
                old   young
these students will be before they die. I would know

seeing as alternative medicine now embraces
the curative powers
                of death   of quarantine
                in a cell

and I've been avoiding being
                assimilated   assassinated
by a public who would have their country
vaccinated in this genocidal way.

The Paranoia Speaks of the Wild

One of my educational exercises exposes the class
to a reading about racism, confusing
the most privileged person in the room. He calls

his parents his slave masters. I start to comment
asking about how much purchasing him cost
but I've already paid the distraction enough

attention. Freedom has been handed down
to the both of us, but I can see
how he has never had to face the price
of living with it. If my depression comes

out of my mouth then suspicions of danger
run rampant around me. If he's discouraged

the wrong statement from me
could set him off, my life becoming a debt
he may aim to collect with the gun
none of us have met yet. I can see the bite

within his resistance towards the reading
in class. He would be taken

in, a misunderstood lone wolf
but a rabid and wild beast nonetheless.

Threats Become Jokes

Cops use their shooting ranges
when they can't just practice
by finding someone of my complexion

to target. Weeks before
being hired at the community college
there was a shooting. Weeks after
being hired at the community college
there was a shooting. There's a hit man

hiding in my blood pressure, an assassin
waiting within the wine

cellar and even my sugar
will eventually take aim
in my direction. Threats become jokes

when everything guns for your existence
and life becomes a classroom where learning
even how much you are worth

to others comes with a cost. Everyday feels like
a training exercise for the moment

when you are announced
as the new face on a t-shirt, the new
picture to be identified

on the news. The new angel
no longer in waiting
hovering overhead like a helicopter.

Sentences

I start off my literature lesson
by asking my pupils to list
who they look to as role models

when they think of entertainers
and musicians. While I'm at the board
a student confesses
to their recreational drug use. I turn around

slowly, wondering
where that came from

as an instructor
across the hall makes a similar statement. My arms
don't tend to swing a gavel, my judgment

stays reserved. Everyone needs an escape
from the prisons we can't see ourselves in.
I don't wish sentences on either of them
but I do wish my student would write better ones.

Hummingbird

I'm better at juggling my markers in the classroom
than my insecurities. My singing stays satirical
since most times I'm not the hummingbird
who I'm pretending to be. Most masters
in academia might consider my existence there
as a mockery. Maybe it's the blackness
or the youth. Probably the stick figures
used when drawing examples and diagrams
on the board. My methods may mirror madness
to the long winded lectures of those who are facing
the twilight which brings retirement but my time
may be brief, like the fluttering of little wings
and in order for my students to learn I have to keep them
engaged to the end like a romantic comedy and they are
the underdogs I'm rooting for through every passing month.

Therapy

After asking my class a question, nobody raises their hand
to answer so I tell them better to shoot their shot

than not. Usually one of two students give it a try,
wrongly replying so often I have nicknamed them

F Curry and Lewrong James. My literature lesson asks them
to think about entertainers, musicians and role models
and while I'm at the board a student confesses
to their recreational drug use. I turn around

slowly, wondering where that came from
as an instructor across the hall makes a similar statement.

My educational exercise exposes the class
to a reading about racism
and the most privileged person in the room

calls his parents his slave masters. I start to comment
asking about how much purchasing him cost
but I've already paid the distraction

enough attention. Everyone in the class laughed
at each of these instances and after letting class out
someone says I should try stand up comedy, unaware

of the therapy of jovially joking, unaware of the sadness
the clown possesses, how too many comedians
shoot their shot, swallow their shots, instead of working out

all of their issues. When teaching I'm also exercising
everything going on in my head, a better musician

than comic. Most times I'm good
at keeping my composure, composer of the cacophony

of emotions I conceal when trying to deal
with the motions of the everyday. I study my notes,
tune out my sadness. I've gotten good at submerging the storm

of my sadness into a symphony of silence
beneath the silliness I use when teaching.
Teaching is an instrument in the orchestra

of my happiness. My country calls my frustration an alibi
for murder, forcing me to digest the prescription of my emotions
but the joy doesn't go down

easy. I keep vomiting up laughter,
adjusting through jesting, making my own medicine

and when the class is learning, able to answer my questions
it's just like music to my ears, silencing the issues in my head.

While Sitting On My Desk

Cops use their shooting ranges
to target targets the same complexion
as me, and all I can do is think back

on all my experiences that led up to
this moment, where my blood pressure

rises like tension, where a student issues
threats in my classroom and the police
with all of their training have been taught
to hit me and spare the student, say it was

an accident, and all I can do is just laugh,
just ease the elevated emotions in the room
or else buckle under the weight of the insanity.

Acknowledgments

The author thanks, appreciates and acknowledges the following publications in which poems from this collection previously appeared:

82 Review: "Battleship", "Handling the Fragile"
Afrikana: "In College I Knew a Guy Who Kept Suggesting that Coffee Would Cure Me", "Dagger"
Allegro Poetry: "Expectations"
A Quiet Courage: "Sink", "The Token", "When Insulted On the Internet By a Racist I Realized This"
Camroc Press Review: "Stand Up Until the Guns Stop"
Emerge Literary Journal: "Anxiety", "Passed Down Practices"
Mobius: The Journal For Social Change: "Letting the Monster Live", "Virtually Deadly"
One Sentence Poems: "The Paranoia Says the Helicopter Searches For Me", "Fear & Forgiveness"
One Throne Magazine: "Today"
Prime Number Magazine: "Pitbull"
Radius: From the Center to the Edge: "Time Capsule"
Scissors and Spackle: "Eulogy to my Grandmother"
Split This Rock: "On the Porch"
The Blueshift Journal: "Orbit"
The Missing Slate: "Barrel"
The This Magazine: "Holden Hall Dorms, 2008" , "Phantom"
Word Riot: "Yearbook"

About the Author

Deonte Osayande is a former track and field sprinter turned writer from Detroit, Mi. He writes nonfiction essays and his poems have been nominated for the Best of the Net Anthology, the Pushcart Prize, and have been published in numerous journals and magazines. Osayande has represented Detroit at multiple National Poetry Slam competitions. He finished third place as an individual poet at the Rustbelt Midwest Regional Poetry Slam. He is the author of multiple chapbooks including most recently **Cover the Sky With Crows** (ELJ Publications 2015). Osayande is currently a professor of English at the University of Detroit Mercy and Wayne County Community College as well as teaches youth through the Inside Out Detroit Literary Arts Program. Class is his first full collection of poetry.

Special Thanks

Aurora Harris and Broadside Lotus Press, for dedicating so much time to my development as a writer, poet and person.

Jessica Care Moore and Moore Black Press, for being an inspiration and always a friend.

ELJ Publications for always being supportive and for running a press like a family.

Chantay Legacy Leonard, for always being a big sister, for being someone I could talk to in my times of need. Rest in Peace.

Omari King Wise Barksdale, for being the big brother I never had, and always looking out for me and putting others before yourself.

My parents for raising me in a house full of love and a love of learning, for teaching me how to be a student and a teacher.

My friends and family for all the support over the years.

Thank you to Hanif Willis Abdurraquib, Clint Smith, Safia Elhillo, Sarah Lawson, Vogue Robinson, AJ Moyer, Will Evans, Scott Woods, John JG the Juggernaut Gibson, Drew Anderson, Dwayne Lawson Brown, Angelique Palmer, Paulie Lipman, Micheal Lee, Samuel Cook, Dylan Garity, Rudy Francisco, Shameca Moore, Jared Paul, Nate Marshall, Chris August, Pages Matam, Amin Drew Law, George Yamazawa, Roscoe Burnems, Michelle Dodd, Mckendy Fils Aime, Tricia Henly, Rachel Mckibbens and the many other poets I've met in my travels, thank you for being the community I didn't know I needed

Thank you to Natasha T Miller, Jeff Nelson, Matthew Lucky Lefty Sawyer, Dimonique Boyd, and the whole Detroit Poetry Community for being an dysfunctional but extended family for me

Justin Rogers, for being my right hand man that I can count on in any situation

Lastly, to my beautiful fiancee Priscilla Garrett, thank you for teaching me so much and helping me grow and develop as a human being and conversely grow as a poet. For always being a friend when I need one. Here's to spending forever with you by my side.

CPSIA information can be obtained
at www.ICGtesting.com
Printed in the USA
LVOW03s0850060418
572513LV00001B/34/P